How Your
BODY
Works

Your
Brain

ACKNOWLEDGMENTS

With thanks to: Imran Akhtar, Kaneesha Watt, Billy Hart, Michael Chin, Inaki Campbell-Arranz, Charlotte Hole, Jessica Ebsworth, and Skye Johnson. Models from The Norrie Carr Agency and Truly Scrumptious Ltd.

Please visit our web site at: www.garethstevens.com
For a free color catalog describing Gareth Stevens Publishing's
list of high-quality books and multimedia programs, call
1-800-542-2595 (USA) or 1-800-387-3178 (Canada).
Gareth Stevens Publishing's fax: (414) 332-3567.

Library of Congress Cataloging-in-Publication Data

Ganeri, Anita, 1961-
    Your brain / by Anita Ganeri.
       p. cm. — (How your body works)
    Summary: An introduction to the structure and function of the human brain and nervous system.
    Includes bibliographical references and index.
    ISBN 0-8368-3632-4 (lib. bdg.)
    1. Brain—Juvenile literature. [1. Brain. 2. Nervous system.] I. Title. II. Series.
QP376.G365   2003
612.8'2—dc21   2002036528

This North American edition first published in 2003 by
Gareth Stevens Publishing
A World Almanac Education Group Company
330 West Olive Street, Suite 100
Milwaukee, WI 53212 USA

Original edition © 2003 by Evans Brothers Limited. First published in 2003 by Evans Brothers Limited, 2A Portman Mansions, Chiltern Street, London W1U 6NR, United Kingdom. This U.S. edition published under license from Evans Brothers Limited. This U.S. edition © 2003 by Gareth Stevens, Inc. Additional end matter © 2003 by Gareth Stevens, Inc.

Designer: Mark Holt
Artwork: Julian Baker; Richard Morgan, page 22.
Photography: Steve Shott
Consultant: Dr. M. Turner

Gareth Stevens Editor: Carol Ryback
Gareth Stevens Designer: Katherine A. Goedheer

Photo credits:
Science Photo Library: Astrid and Hanns-Frieder Michler, page 7; Volker-Steger, page 8; CNRI, page 16; BSIP, Laurent/Gluck, page 23; Philippe Plailly, page 24.

Printed in the United States of America

1 2 3 4 5 6 7 8 9 07 06 05 04 03

Contents

Brain Power

Your brain is amazing. It is like a computer hidden inside your head. It lets you think, learn, and remember. Your brain controls every part of your body. It makes you understand and feel what is happening, using messages sent from the rest of your body. These messages zoom around your body through long, thin fibers called **nerves**. Your brain sorts the messages and tells your body what to do. Together, your brain and your nerves form a network called the **nervous system**.

Amazing!

As you read, your eyes send messages to your brain about the words and pictures. Then your brain helps you make sense of what you are reading.

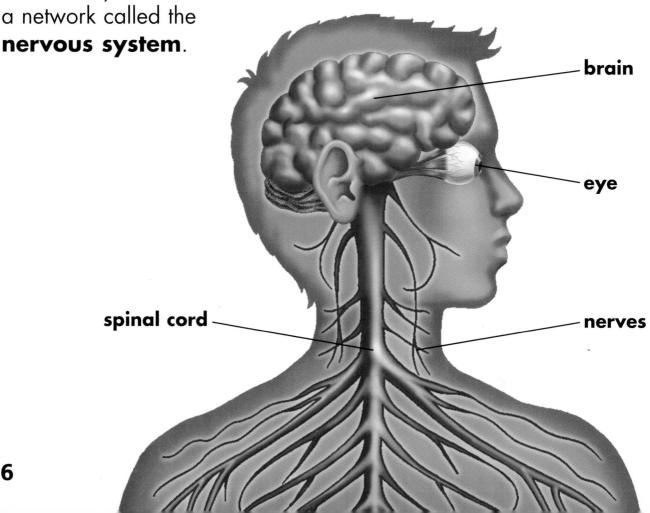

brain

eye

spinal cord

nerves

Your brain is the most important part of your body. Without it, your body could not work. Your brain sits inside a hard, bony case called a **skull**. It has many bones that fit together like jigsaw puzzle pieces.

Your bony skull protects your delicate brain.

You might think that smarter people have larger brains, but everyone's brain is about the same size.

Your Amazing Brain

Your amazing brain fits snugly inside your skull in the top half of your head. It looks like a folded, wrinkled mass of fat noodles! An adult's brain weighs about 3 pounds (1.5 kilograms) — about as much as six large oranges.

Your brain automatically keeps your heart and lungs working without you even thinking about it.

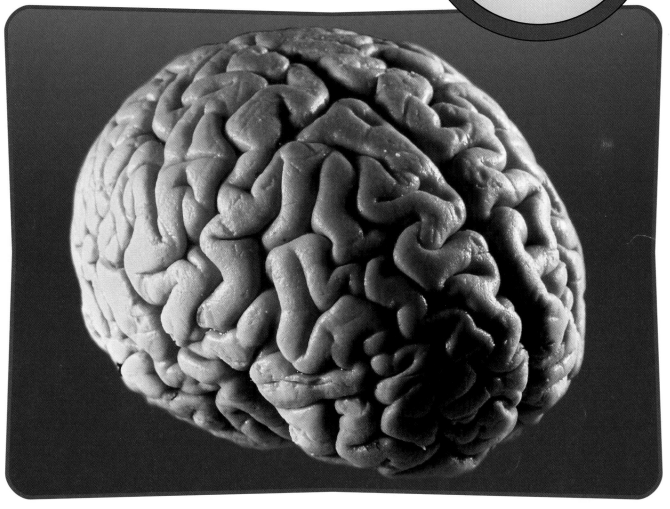

The surface of a human brain is covered in wrinkles.

8

Your brain is made of billions of nerve **cells**. These nerve cells send messages around your body. Each nerve cell can "talk" to many other nerves, forming a huge nerve network. To work properly, your brain needs a good blood supply with lots of **oxygen** and **nutrients**. Tiny tubes called **blood vessels** carry the oxygen and nutrients to your brain.

Amazing!

Your busy brain can store as much information as a set of twenty encyclopedias.

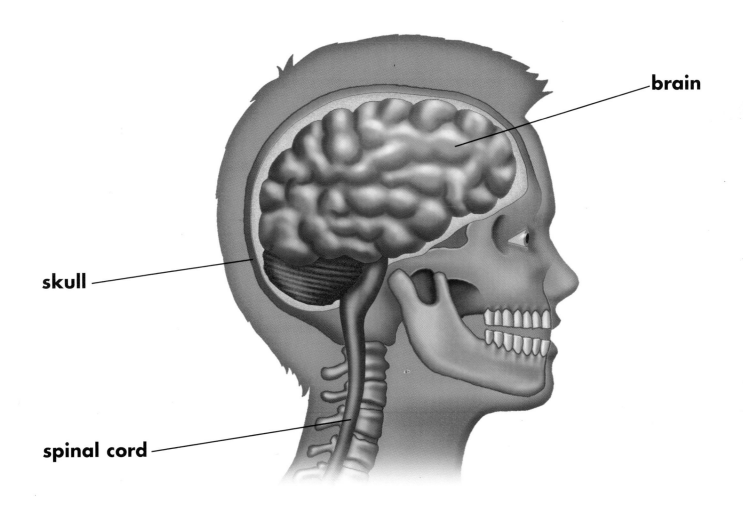

brain

skull

spinal cord

Brain Map

Each area of your brain controls a different set of nerve messages. For example, your eyes send messages to the brain area near the back of your head. The brain map below shows different messages and the areas of your brain that control them.

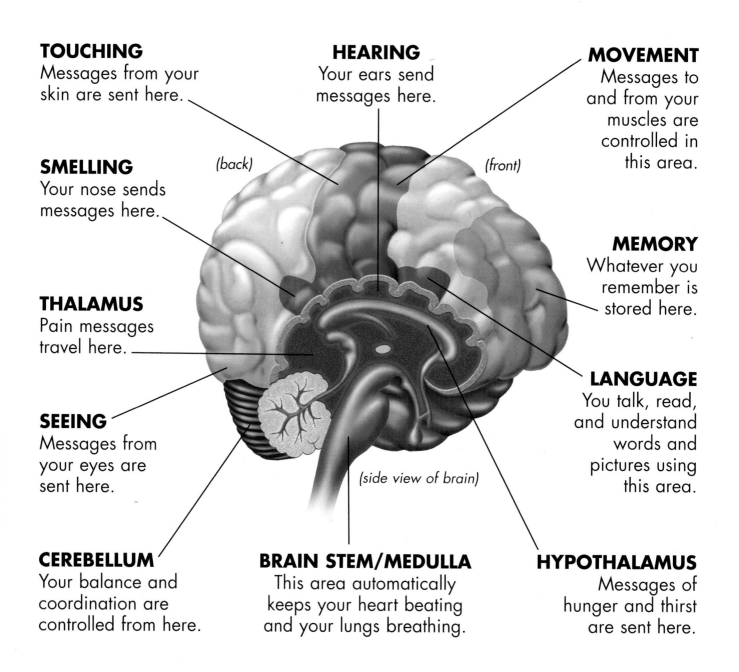

TOUCHING
Messages from your skin are sent here.

HEARING
Your ears send messages here.

MOVEMENT
Messages to and from your muscles are controlled in this area.

SMELLING
Your nose sends messages here.

(back)

(front)

MEMORY
Whatever you remember is stored here.

THALAMUS
Pain messages travel here.

LANGUAGE
You talk, read, and understand words and pictures using this area.

SEEING
Messages from your eyes are sent here.

(side view of brain)

CEREBELLUM
Your balance and coordination are controlled from here.

BRAIN STEM/MEDULLA
This area automatically keeps your heart beating and your lungs breathing.

HYPOTHALAMUS
Messages of hunger and thirst are sent here.

Your brain sorts through nerve messages and keeps only the most important information.

Amazing!

Every day, thousands of your brain cells die and cannot be replaced. But don't worry — you have billions of them.

Left Brain, Right Brain

Your brain has two sides. The left side of your brain controls the right side of your body. The right side of your brain controls the left side of your body. Each side of your brain also controls different skills and activities. The left side of your brain controls activities that need careful thinking, such as doing math or playing a game of chess. The right side of your brain controls artistic activities, such as painting or playing a musical instrument.

Amazing!

Over 200 million nerves join the two sides of your brain. These nerves pass messages from the left side to the right side and back again.

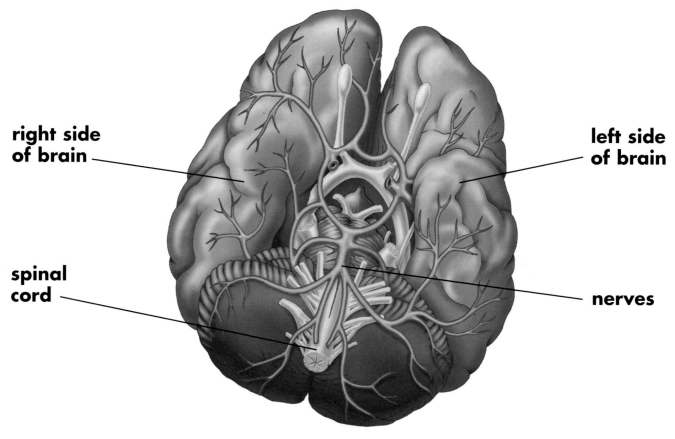

right side of brain

left side of brain

spinal cord

nerves

(view of brain from underneath)

Are you left-handed or right-handed? The hand you write with depends on which side of your brain controls your language and speaking. In right-handed people, the left side of the brain is in charge. In left-handed people, the right side is in charge. Some people are **ambidextrous,** which means they can write with both hands.

Try writing your name with the opposite hand that you normally use. See how difficult it is?

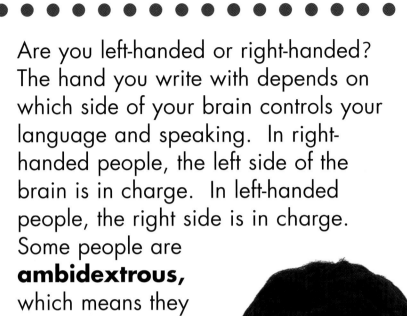

What a Nerve!

Your nerves are like long, thin threads that run through your body. They carry messages to and from your brain. When your arm itches, nerves in your skin send a message to your brain. Your brain notices the itch and sends a message back to your hand, telling it to scratch the itch.

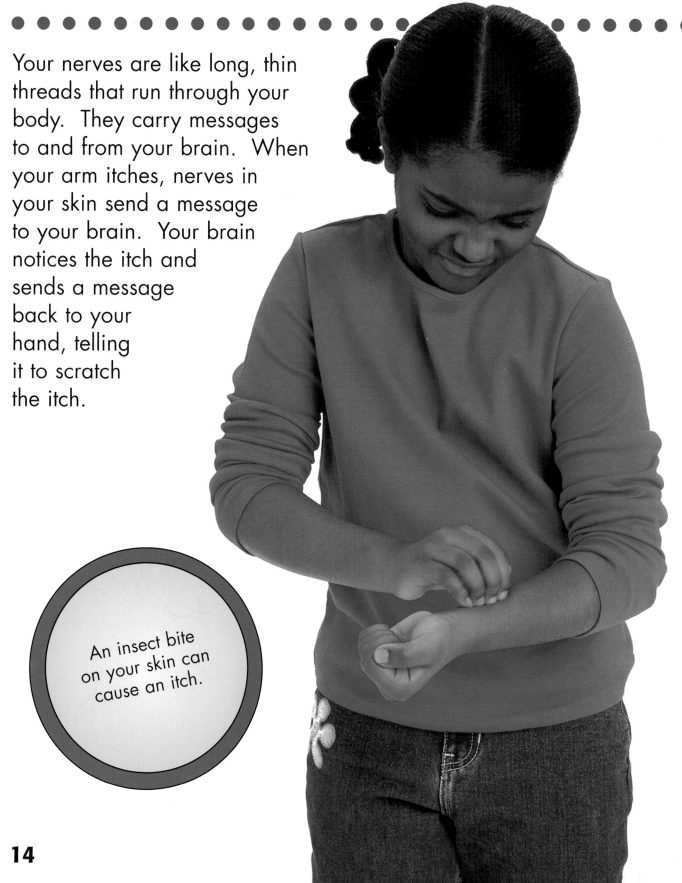

An insect bite on your skin can cause an itch.

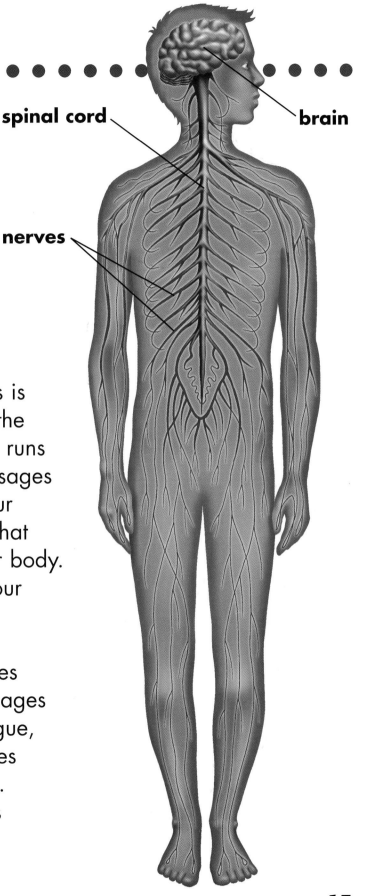

spinal cord

brain

nerves

The main pathway for messages is
a thick bundle of nerves called the
spinal cord. Your spinal cord runs
through your **backbone**. Messages
from your brain travel down your
spinal cord, then along nerves that
branch out to every part of your body.
Messages also travel back to your
brain from all over your body.

You have over 100 million nerves
in your body. Some carry messages
from your eyes, ears, nose, tongue,
and skin. Others carry messages
from your brain to your muscles.
Still more nerves pass messages
between the nerves themselves.

How Nerves Work

Your nerves are made from strings of nerve cells that look like tiny threads or wires. Nerve cells are so tiny you can see them only with a **microscope**. Even though nerve cells are tiny, they can be very long. In fact, they can be as much as a yard (meter) long.

Amazing!

Some messages whiz along your nerves at very high speeds — even faster than "warp" speed.

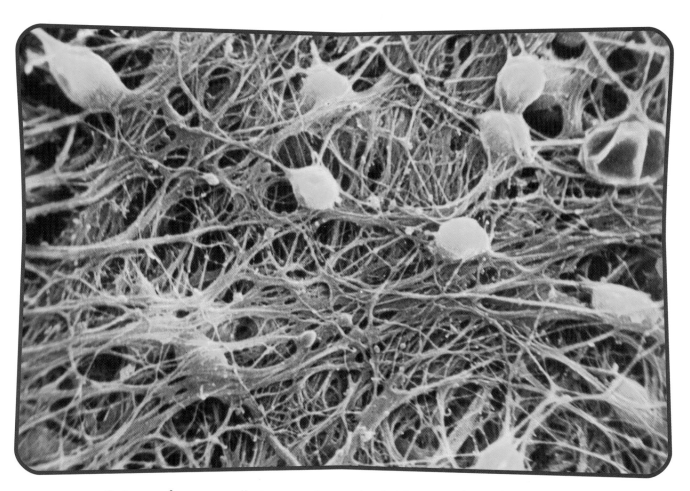

Strings of nerve cells in your brain look like tiny threads or wires.

Your nerve cells do not touch each other. They have tiny gaps, or spaces, between them. Messages must "jump" across these gaps to travel from one nerve cell to another.

How do your nerves work? When you stub your toe, your toe nerves send messages through your body to your brain. Your brain makes you feel the pain. Ouch!

Stubbing your toe is painful but very useful. Pain is your body's warning system. Pain warns you to stop. Something is in your way.

Pain signals travel to your brain faster than touch signals. When you stub your toe, you feel the pain within a second.

Quick Reactions

If you prick your finger on a pin, you pull your hand away immediately — without even thinking about it. This movement is called a **reflex action**. It helps protect your body from danger. Usually, your nerves send a message to your brain, then your brain sends a message to your muscles, telling them to move. In a reflex action, your nerves send a message directly to your muscles, telling them to move right away.

Cross your legs and gently tap your knee just under your kneecap. If your leg jerks, you know your reflexes are working.

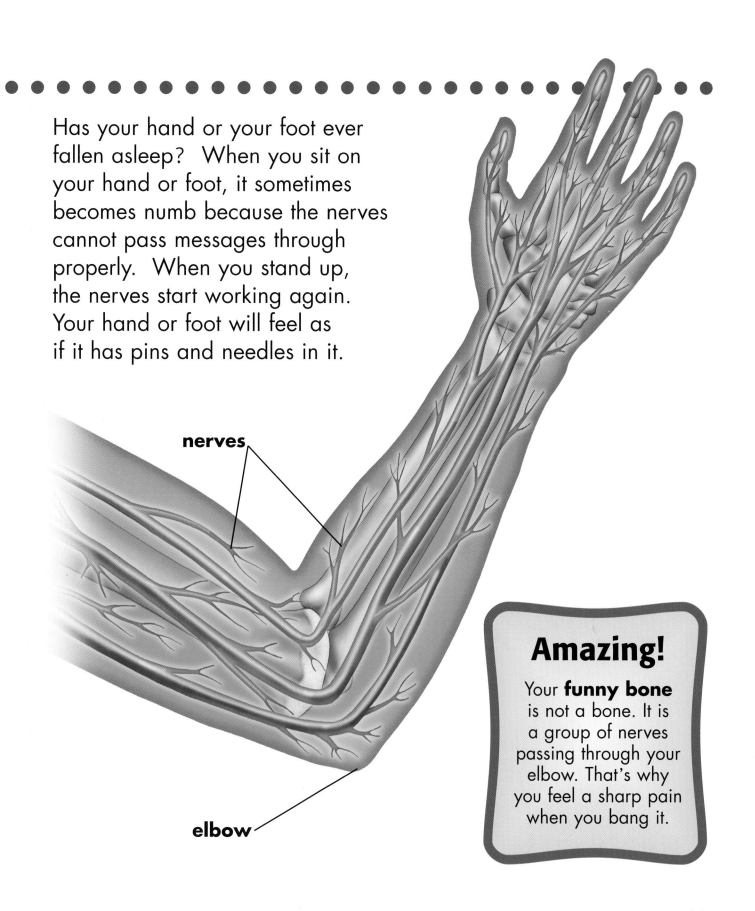

Has your hand or your foot ever fallen asleep? When you sit on your hand or foot, it sometimes becomes numb because the nerves cannot pass messages through properly. When you stand up, the nerves start working again. Your hand or foot will feel as if it has pins and needles in it.

nerves

elbow

Amazing!

Your **funny bone** is not a bone. It is a group of nerves passing through your elbow. That's why you feel a sharp pain when you bang it.

Learning a Lesson

You keep learning all your life. Learning a new lesson makes your brain work, think, and remember. When your teacher writes a math problem on the board, your eyes see it and send the problem to your amazing brain. Your brain figures out the problem, then sends a message to your hand to write down the answer. Your brain can store that math lesson in your memory for many, many years.

Amazing!

A person who remembers what is on a page as if he or she were looking at a photograph of that page has a **photographic memory**.

As you learn, your brain stores information as **memories**. But your brain cannot remember everything — it would run out of room. You remember important things, such as your first day at school. You forget less important things, such as what you had for lunch.

Test your memory. Look at 10 objects on a tray for 15 seconds, then look away. Now try to remember as many objects as you can.

Sweet Dreams

Dreams are pictures or stories your brain makes up while you are asleep. Even though they are not really happening, dreams often feel very real. They may be linked to things that happened during the day. You might dream about a TV program you watched or about something you read. Some dreams are very unusual. Other dreams are very scary. Scary dreams are called **nightmares**. But don't worry — nightmares stop when you wake up.

Amazing!

A special machine can record your brain activity as you dream. The dreams appear as squiggy lines on the machine's monitor.

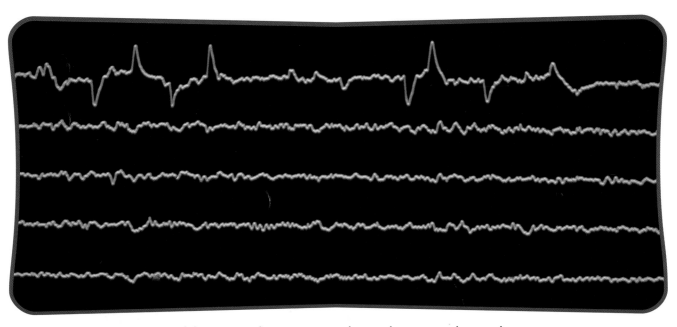

Jagged lines on the monitor show that your brain keeps working even when you are sleeping and dreaming.

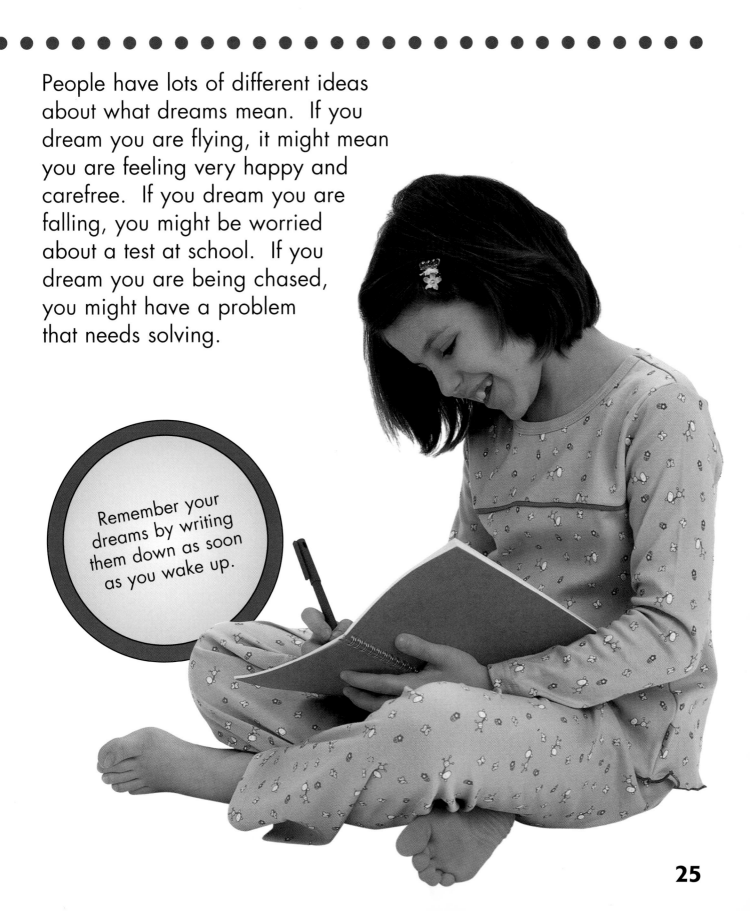

People have lots of different ideas about what dreams mean. If you dream you are flying, it might mean you are feeling very happy and carefree. If you dream you are falling, you might be worried about a test at school. If you dream you are being chased, you might have a problem that needs solving.

Remember your dreams by writing them down as soon as you wake up.

Activity

Your brain is divided into different areas. How many areas can you name? Photocopy page 27. Match the numbers below to the brain areas listed on page 27.

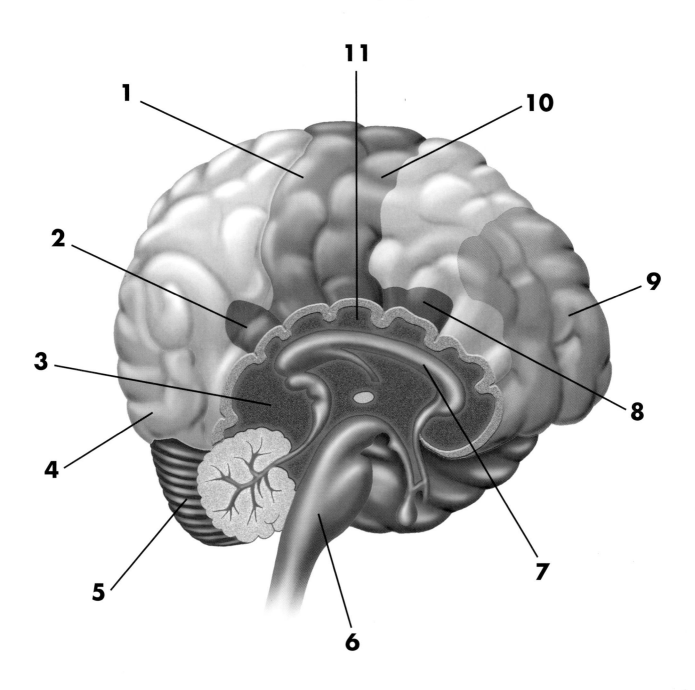

_____ **thalamus**

_____ **memory**

_____ **smelling**

_____ **seeing**

_____ **cerebellum**

_____ **brain stem/medulla**

_____ **hypothalamus**

_____ **touching**

_____ **language**

_____ **hearing**

_____ **movement**

Glossary

ambidextrous: having the ability to use your right hand or your left hand equally well.

backbone: a column of twenty-six connected bones that runs down your back.

blood vessels: soft, flexible "tubes" that carry blood to all parts of your body.

brain stem: the area where your spinal cord is connected to your brain.

cells: the tiny pieces of living matter that form your muscles, bones, lungs, eyes, and other parts of your body.

cerebellum: the area near your brain stem that controls how well your muscles work together. It automatically helps you keep your balance and steady yourself.

digesting: breaking down food into tiny pieces that your blood can carry through your entire body.

funny bone: a group of nerves in your elbow that gives you a sharp pain when you bang it.

hypothalamus: the area of your brain that works automatically to control hunger and thirst. It also keeps your body at the correct temperature.

medulla: the area of your brain stem that controls your heartbeat and rate of breathing.

memories: the sights, sounds, smells, or feelings from the past that you can remember just by thinking. You make new memories all your life.

microscope: an instrument used to look at objects that are too tiny to see with just your eyes.

nerves: special cells that look like thin threads or wires and carry messages between your body and your brain.

nervous system: the network formed by your brain and all the nerves in your body.

nightmares: bad dreams.

nutrients: tiny pieces of food that are carried around your body by your blood.

oxygen: a gas in the air that you need to breathe.

photographic memory: the ability to remember things as clearly as if you were looking at photographs of them.

reflex action: a movement that happens automatically, such as pulling your hand away quickly when you touch something that is very hot.

skull: the hard bones that form your head and protect your brain from injury.

spinal cord: the thick bundle of nerves that runs down your back inside the bones of your spine, or backbone.

thalamus: the area in your brain that passes messages between your brain and your spinal cord. Pain messages from your body travel here.

More Books to Read

The Brain: Our Nervous System.
    Seymour Simon
    (William Morrow)

The Human Brain. Marcus
    Barbor (Running Press)

The Science of the Senses.
    Living Science (series).
    Patricia Miller-Schroeder
    (Gareth Stevens)

Understanding Your Brain.
    Science for Beginners (series).
    Rebecca Treays (EDC)

*Why Do I Get a Toothache: And
    Other Questions about Nerves.*
    Body Matters (series). Angela
    Royston (Heinemann Library)

Your Brain. Terri Degezelle
    (Bridgestone Books)

Videos

All About the Brain.
    (Schlessinger Media)

It's All In Your Head.
    (Bill Young Productions)

Web Sites

The Brain Is the Boss.
    www.kidshealth.org/kid/body/
    brain_noSW.html

BrainPOP: Nervous System.
    www.brainpop.com/health/
    nervous/brain/

Index